Life Lessons

from THE INSPIRED WORD of GOD

BOOKS of
1 & 2 PETER

MAX LUCADO

General Editor

TABLE OF CONTENTS

HOW TO STUDY THE BIBLE

BY MAX LUCADO

*T*his is a peculiar book you are holding. Words crafted in another language. Deeds done in a distant era. Events recorded in a far-off land. Counsel offered to a foreign people. This is a peculiar book.

It's surprising that anyone reads it. It's too old. Some of its writings date back five thousand years. It's too bizarre. The book speaks of incredible floods, fires, earthquakes, and people with supernatural abilities. It's too radical. The Bible calls for undying devotion to a carpenter who called himself God's Son.

Logic says this book shouldn't survive. Too old, too bizarre, too radical.

The Bible has been banned, burned, scoffed, and ridiculed. Scholars have mocked it as foolish. Kings have branded it as illegal. A thousand times over it the grave has been dug and the dirge has begun, but somehow the Bible never stays in the grave. Not only has it survived, it has thrived. It is the single most popular book in all of history. It has been the best-selling book in the world for years!

There is no way on earth to explain it. Which perhaps is the only explanation. The answer? The Bible's durability is not found on earth; it is found in heaven. For the millions who have tested its claims and claimed its promises, there is but one answer—the Bible is God's book and God's voice.

As you read it, you would be wise to give some thought to two questions. What is the purpose of the Bible? and How do I study the Bible? Time spent reflecting on these two issues will greatly enhance your Bible study.

What is the purpose of the Bible?

Let the Bible itself answer that question.

Since you were a child you have known the Holy Scriptures which are able to make you wise. And that wisdom leads to salvation through faith in Christ Jesus.

(2 Tim. 3:15)

The purpose of the Bible? Salvation. God's highest passion is to get his children home. His book, the Bible, describes his plan of salvation. The purpose of the Bible is to proclaim God's plan and passion to save his children.

That is the reason this book has endured through the centuries. It dares to tackle the toughest questions about life: Where do I go after I die? Is there a God? What do I do with my fears? The Bible offers answers to these crucial questions. It is the treasure map that leads us to God's highest treasure, eternal life.

But how do we use the Bible? Countless copies of Scripture sit unread on bookshelves and nightstands simply because people don't know how to read it. What can we do to make the Bible real in our lives?

The clearest answer is found in the words of Jesus.

"Ask," he promised, *"and God will give to you. Search, and you will find. Knock, and the door will open for you."*

(Matt. 7:7)

The first step in understanding the Bible is asking God to help us. We should read prayerfully. If anyone understands God's Word, it is because of God and not the reader.

But the Helper will teach you everything and will cause you to remember all that I told you. The Helper is the Holy Spirit whom the Father will send in my name.

(John 14:26)

Before reading the Bible, pray. Invite God to speak to you. Don't go to Scripture looking for your idea; go searching for his.

Not only should we read the Bible prayerfully, we should read it carefully. *Search and you will find* is the pledge. The Bible is not a newspaper to be skimmed but rather a mine to be quarried. *Search for it like silver, and hunt for it like hidden treasure. Then you will understand respect for the LORD, and you will find that you know God* (Prov. 2:4).

Any worthy find requires effort. The Bible is no exception. To understand the Bible you don't have to be brilliant, but you must be willing to roll up your sleeves and search.

Be a worker who is not ashamed and who uses the true teaching in the right way.

(2 Tim. 2:15)

Here's a practical point. Study the Bible a bit at a time. Hunger is not satisfied by eating twenty-one meals in one sitting once a week. The body needs a steady diet to remain strong. So does the soul. When God sent food to his people in the wilderness, he didn't provide loaves already made. Instead, he sent them manna in the shape of *thin flakes like frost . . . on the desert ground* (Exod. 16:14).

God gave manna in limited portions.

God sends spiritual food the same way. He opens the heavens with just enough nutrients for today's hunger. He provides, *a command here, a command there. A rule here, a rule there. A little lesson here, a little lesson there* (Isa. 28:10).

Don't be discouraged if your reading reaps a small harvest. Some days a lesser portion is all that is needed. What is important is to search every day for that day's message. A steady diet of God's Word over a lifetime builds a healthy soul and mind.

A little girl returned from her first day at school. Her mom asked, "Did you learn anything?" "Apparently not enough," the girl responded, "I have to go back tomorrow and the next day and the next. . . ."

Such is the case with learning. And such is the case with Bible study. Understanding comes little by little over a lifetime.

There is a third step in understanding the Bible. After the asking and seeking comes the knocking. After you ask and search, then knock.

Knock, and the door will open for you.
(Matt. 7:7)

To knock is to stand at God's door. To make yourself available. To climb the steps, cross the porch, stand at the doorway, and volunteer. Knocking goes beyond the realm of thinking and into the realm of acting.

To knock is to ask, What can I do? How can I obey? Where can I go?

It's one thing to know what to do. It's another to do it. But for those who do it, those who choose to obey, a special reward awaits them.

The truly happy people are those who carefully study God's perfect law that makes people free, and they continue to study it. They do not forget what they heard, but they obey what God's teaching says. Those who do this will be made happy.
(James 1:25)

What a promise! Happiness comes to those who do what they read! It's the same with medicine. If you only read the label but ignore the pills, it won't help. It's the same with food. If you only read the recipe but never cook, you won't be fed. And it's the same with the Bible. If you only read the words but never obey, you'll never know the joy God has promised.

Ask. Search. Knock. Simple, isn't it? Why don't you give it a try? If you do, you'll see why you are holding the most remarkable book in history.

1 PETER

INTRODUCTION

*I*t's not easy being the only one in your family who goes to church. It's bad enough that they don't go. It's worse that they make fun of you for going. If you would pad your expense account, so could the other salesmen. But if you don't, they can't. "Come on," they urge you, "just hedge a little." You refuse. The next day someone has spilled paint on your car.

Persecution. Not by firing squad. Not by death threats. Not by the government. But it's persecution nonetheless. A more subtle persecution. Persecution from friends, family, and peers. They won't take your life . . . but they will take your peace . . . and they'd like to take your faith, if you'll let them.

How do you respond? Begin with Peter's survival manual. He understood persecution. Beaten and jailed. Threatened and punished. He knew the sting of the false word and the angry whip. No doubt he'd seen some Christians stand and others fall. He'd seen enough to know what it takes to stay strong in tough times.

His counsel may surprise you.

His counsel may sustain you. It may be just what you need so that "the purity of your faith will bring you praise and glory and honor when Jesus Christ is shown to you" (1:7).

LESSON ONE

A LIVING HOPE

REFLECTION

Begin your study by sharing thoughts on this question.

1. Think of a time when you felt hopeless about a situation in your life. How did you cope?

_____

_____

_____

BIBLE READING

Read 1 Peter 1:1–12 from the NCV or the NKJV.

NCV	NKJV
¹From Peter, an apostle of Jesus Christ.	Peter, an apostle of Jesus Christ,
To God's chosen people who are away from their homes and are scattered all around the countries of Pontus, Galatia, Cappadocia, Asia, and Bithynia. ²God planned long ago to choose you by making you his holy people, which is the Spirit's work. God wanted you to obey him and to be made clean by the blood of the death of Jesus Christ.	¹To the pilgrims of the Dispersion in Pontus, Galatia, Cappadocia, Asia, and Bithynia, ²elect according to the foreknowledge of God the Father, in sanctification of the Spirit, for obedience and sprinkling of the blood of Jesus Christ:
Grace and peace be yours more and more.	Grace to you and peace be multiplied.

NCV

[3]Praise be to the God and Father of our Lord Jesus Christ. In God's great mercy he has caused us to be born again into a living hope, because Jesus Christ rose from the dead. [4]Now we hope for the blessings God has for his children. These blessings, which cannot be destroyed or be spoiled or lose their beauty, are kept in heaven for you. [5]God's power protects you through your faith until salvation is shown to you at the end of time. [6]This makes you very happy, even though now for a short time different kinds of troubles may make you sad. [7]These troubles come to prove that your faith is pure. This purity of faith is worth more than gold, which can be proved to be pure by fire but will ruin. But the purity of your faith will bring you praise and glory and honor when Jesus Christ is shown to you. [8]You have not seen Christ, but still you love him. You cannot see him now, but you believe in him. So you are filled with a joy that cannot be explained, a joy full of glory. [9]And you are receiving the goal of your faith—the salvation of your souls.

[10]The prophets searched carefully and tried to learn about this salvation. They prophesied about the grace that was coming to you. [11]The Spirit of Christ was in the prophets, telling in advance about the sufferings of Christ and about the glory that would follow those sufferings. The prophets tried to learn about what the Spirit was showing them, when those things would happen, and what the world would be like at that time. [12]It was shown them that their service was not for themselves but for you, when they told about the truths you have now heard. Those who preached the Good News to

NKJV

[3]Blessed *be* the God and Father of our Lord Jesus Christ, who according to His abundant mercy has begotten us again to a living hope through the resurrection of Jesus Christ from the dead, [4]to an inheritance incorruptible and undefiled and that does not fade away, reserved in heaven for you, [5]who are kept by the power of God through faith for salvation ready to be revealed in the last time.

[6]In this you greatly rejoice, though now for a little while, if need be, you have been grieved by various trials, [7]that the genuineness of your faith, *being* much more precious than gold that perishes, though it is tested by fire, may be found to praise, honor, and glory at the revelation of Jesus Christ, [8]whom having not seen you love. Though now you do not see *Him,* yet believing, you rejoice with joy inexpressible and full of glory, [9]receiving the end of your faith—the salvation of *your* souls.

[10]Of this salvation the prophets have inquired and searched carefully, who prophesied of the grace *that would come* to you, [11]searching what, or what manner of time, the Spirit of Christ who was in them was indicating when He testified beforehand the sufferings of Christ and the glories that would follow. [12]To them it was revealed that, not to themselves, but to us they were ministering the things which now have been reported to you through those who have preached the gospel to you by the Holy Spirit sent from heaven—things which angels desire to look into.

NCV

you told you those things with the help of the Holy Spirit who was sent from heaven—things into which angels desire to look.

NKJV

DISCOVERY

Explore the Bible reading by discussing these questions.

2. What does it mean to our everyday lives that God plans to make us holy?

_____

_____

_____

3. In what ways do you consider your salvation "a blessing"?

_____

_____

_____

4. How would you describe a pure faith?

_____

_____

_____

5. How can our hope in Jesus help us endure trials?

_____

_____

_____

6. In what way have the trials in your life strengthened your faith?

_____

_____

_____

INSPIRATION

Here is an uplifting thought from *The Inspirational Study Bible*.

There is something about a living testimony that gives us courage. Once we see someone else emerging from life's dark tunnels we realize that we, too, can overcome.

Could this be why Jesus is called our pioneer? Is this one of the reasons that he consented to enter the horrid chambers of death? It must be. His words, though persuasive, were not enough. His promises, though true, didn't quite allay the fear of the people. His actions, even the act of calling Lazarus from the tomb, didn't convince the crowds that death was nothing to fear. No. In the eyes of humanity, death was still the black veil that separated them from joy. There was no victory over this hooded foe. Its putrid odor invaded the nostrils of every human, convincing them that life was only meant to end abruptly and senselessly.

It was left to the Son of God to disclose the true nature of this force. It was on the cross that the showdown occurred. Christ called for Satan's cards. Weary of seeing humanity fooled by a coverup, he entered the tunnel of death to prove that there was indeed an exit. And, as the world darkened, creation held her breath.

Satan threw his best punch, but it wasn't enough. Even the darkness of hell's tunnel was no match for God's Son. Even the chambers of Hades couldn't stop this Raider. Legions of screaming demons held nothing over the Lion of Judah.

Christ emerged from death's tunnel, lifted a triumphant fist toward the sky, and freed all from the fear of death.

"Death has been swallowed up in victory!"

(From *On the Anvil*
by Max Lucado)

RESPONSE

Use these questions to share more deeply with each other.

7. What are some ways that Christ's victory over death encourages you?

_____

_____

_____

8. How would your life be different if Christ had not conquered death?

_____

_____

_____

9. In what way does your hope for the future change the way you live each day?

_____

_____

_____

PRAYER

Father, help us see the joy that is before us. You have given us such a great treasure—the promise of salvation. Forgive us, Father, for losing sight of our glorious future. Renew our vision and help us strain toward the goal of our faith—the salvation of our souls. And when we face trials, remind us that you have won the ultimate victory.

JOURNALING

Take a few moments to record your personal insights from this lesson.

What are the blessings God has given me?

ADDITIONAL QUESTIONS

10. What does it mean to rejoice in your salvation?

_____

_____

_____

11. How does this passage affect your attitude toward the trials in your life?

_____

_____

_____

12. What words of hope from this passage do you want to remember the next time you face trials?

_____

_____

_____

For more Bible passages on hope, see Psalm 42:5; 130:7; Proverbs 23:17–18; Jeremiah 29:11; Romans 8:24–25; 15:4, 13; 1 Corinthians 15:19–32; Colossians 1:27; 1 Thessalonians 1:3; Titus 1:2; 2:11–13; Hebrews 10:23.

To complete the Books of 1 & 2 Peter during this twelve-part study, read 1 Peter 1:1–12.

ADDITIONAL THOUGHTS

LESSON TWO

NEW LIFE IN CHRIST

REFLECTION

Begin your study by sharing thoughts on this question.

1. Think of your lifestyle before you became a Christian. How is your life different now?

_____

_____

_____

BIBLE READING

Read 1 Peter 1:13–25 from the NCV or the NKJV.

NCV

¹³So prepare your minds for service and have self-control. All your hope should be for the gift of grace that will be yours when Jesus Christ is shown to you. ¹⁴Now that you are obedient children of God do not live as you did in the past. You did not understand, so you did the evil things you wanted. ¹⁵But be holy in all you do, just as God, the One who called you, is holy. ¹⁶It is written in the Scriptures: "You must be holy, because I am holy."

¹⁷You pray to God and call him Father, and

NKJV

¹³Therefore gird up the loins of your mind, be sober, and rest *your* hope fully upon the grace that is to be brought to you at the revelation of Jesus Christ; ¹⁴as obedient children, not conforming yourselves to the former lusts, *as* in your ignorance; ¹⁵but as He who called you *is* holy, you also be holy in all *your* conduct, ¹⁶because it is written, "*Be holy, for I am holy.*"

¹⁷And if you call on the Father, who without partiality judges according to each one's work, conduct yourselves throughout the time of

NCV

he judges each person's work equally. So while you are here on earth, you should live with respect for God. [18]You know that in the past you were living in a worthless way, a way passed down from the people who lived before you. But you were saved from that useless life. You were bought, not with something that ruins like gold or silver, [19]but with the precious blood of Christ, who was like a pure and perfect lamb. [20]Christ was chosen before the world was made, but he was shown to the world in these last times for your sake. [21]Through Christ you believe in God, who raised Christ from the dead and gave him glory. So your faith and your hope are in God.

[22]Now that you have made your souls pure by obeying the truth, you can have true love for your Christian brothers and sisters. So love each other deeply with all your heart. [23]You have been born again, and this new life did not come from something that dies, but from something that cannot die. You were born again through God's living message that continues forever. [24]The Scripture says,

"All people are like the grass,
and all their glory is like the flowers of
the field.
The grass dies and the flowers fall,
[25]but the word of the Lord will live
forever."
And this is the word that was preached to you.

NKJV

your stay *here* in fear; [18]knowing that you were not redeemed with corruptible things, *like* silver or gold, from your aimless conduct *received* by tradition from your fathers, [19]but with the precious blood of Christ, as of a lamb without blemish and without spot. [20]He indeed was foreordained before the foundation of the world, but was manifest in these last times for you [21]who through Him believe in God, who raised Him from the dead and gave Him glory, so that your faith and hope are in God.

[22]Since you have purified your souls in obeying the truth through the Spirit in sincere love of the brethren, love one another fervently with a pure heart, [23]having been born again, not of corruptible seed but incorruptible, through the word of God which lives and abides forever, [24]because

" All flesh *is* as grass,
And all the glory of man as the flower of
the grass.
The grass withers,
And its flower falls away,
[25] But the word of the LORD endures forever."

Now this is the word which by the gospel was preached to you.

DISCOVERY

Explore the Bible reading by discussing these questions.

2. How do our lives change after conversion?

_____

_____

_____

3. What does it mean to be holy?

_____

_____

_____

4. What motivates us to live righteously?

_____

_____

_____

5. Why is it important to understand the price Jesus paid for our salvation?

_____

_____

_____

6. This passage says that being pure enables us to demonstrate true love to others. What is the relationship between being pure and showing love?

_____

_____

_____

INSPIRATION

Here is an uplifting thought from *The Inspirational Study Bible*.

Jesus told us we must be born again. The infinitive *be* is passive. It shows that it is something that must be done for us. No man can "born" himself. He must be born. The new birth is wholly foreign to our will. In other words, the new birth is a divine work—we are born of God.

Even though the new birth seems mysterious, that does not make it untrue. We may not understand the how of electricity, but we know that it lights our homes, runs our television and radio sets. We do not understand how the sheep grows wool, the cow grows hair, or the fowl grows feathers—but we know they do. We do not understand many mysteries, but we accept by faith the fact that at the moment we repent of sin and turn by faith to Jesus Christ we are born again.

It is the infusion of divine life into the human soul. It is the implementation or impartation of divine nature into the human soul whereby we become the children of God. We receive the breath of God. Christ through the Holy Spirit takes up residence in our hearts. We are attached to God for eternity. That means that if you have been born again, you will live as long as God lives, because you are now sharing His very life. The long-lost fellowship man had with God in the Garden of Eden has been restored. . . .

This new nature that you receive from God is bent to the will of God. You will want to do only His will. You are utterly and completely devoted to Him. There is a new self-determination, inclination, disposition, a new principle of living, new choices. You seek to glorify God. You seek fellowship with other Christians in the church. You love the Bible. You love to spend time in prayer with God. Your whole disposition is changed. Whereas your life once was filled with unbelief, the root and foundation of all sin, and you once doubted God, now you believe Him. Now you have utmost confidence and faith in God and His Word.

(From *Peace with God*
by Billy Graham)

RESPONSE

Use these questions to share more deeply with each other.

7. Were there any insights from this passage about spiritual rebirth that were new to you?

_____

_____

_____

8. How would you explain what it means to be born again to a friend with no religious background?

_____

_____

_____

9. Who helped you realize your need for a spiritual rebirth?

_____

_____

_____

PRAYER

Father, we thank you for the gift of grace that is ours through Jesus Christ. We claim your salvation and ask you to help us respond with humility and obedience. Father, you have commanded us to be holy, just as you are holy. But we can do nothing without you. So we ask you to work through us, by your Spirit, and transform us into your likeness.

JOURNALING

Take a few moments to record your personal insights from this lesson.

What evidence of new life in Christ can I see in myself?

ADDITIONAL QUESTIONS

10. In what ways do we sometimes trivialize Christ's sacrifice?

_____

_____

_____

11. Why is it difficult to change our ways after we are born again?

_____

_____

_____

12. What old habits have you needed God's help to give up?

_____

_____

_____

For more Bible passages on spiritual rebirth, see John 3:3–8; 2 Corinthians 5:17; Galatians 6:15; Ephesians 2:4–10; Titus 3:3–7; 1 Peter 1:3; 1 John 3:9.

To complete the Books of 1 & 2 Peter during this twelve-part study, read 1 Peter 1:13–25.

ADDITIONAL THOUGHTS

LESSON THREE

JESUS CHRIST, THE CORNERSTONE

REFLECTION

Begin your study by sharing thoughts on this statement.

1. Think of a time when you re-established a relationship with a long-lost friend. Describe your feelings at that time.

_____

_____

_____

BIBLE READING

Read 1 Peter 2:1–10 from the NCV or the NKJV.

NCV

¹So then, rid yourselves of all evil, all lying, hypocrisy, jealousy, and evil speech. ²As new-born babies want milk, you should want the pure and simple teaching. By it you can grow up and be saved, ³because you have already examined and seen how good the Lord is.

⁴Come to the Lord Jesus, the "stone" that lives. The people of the world did not want this stone, but he was the stone God chose, and he was precious. ⁵You also are like living stones, so

NKJV

¹Therefore, laying aside all malice, all deceit, hypocrisy, envy, and all evil speaking, ²as new-born babes, desire the pure milk of the word, that you may grow thereby, ³if indeed you have tasted that the Lord *is* gracious.

⁴Coming to Him *as to* a living stone, reject-ed indeed by men, but chosen by God *and* precious, ⁵you also, as living stones, are being built up a spiritual house, a holy priesthood, to offer up spiritual sacrifices acceptable to

NCV

let yourselves be used to build a spiritual temple—to be holy priests who offer spiritual sacrifices to God. He will accept those sacrifices through Jesus Christ. [6]The Scripture says:

> "I will put a stone in the ground in
> Jerusalem.
> Everything will be built on this
> important and precious rock.
> Anyone who trusts in him
> will never be disappointed."

[7]This stone is worth much to you who believe. But to the people who do not believe,

> "the stone that the builders rejected
> has become the cornerstone."

[8]Also, he is

> "a stone that causes people to stumble,
> a rock that makes them fall."

They stumble because they do not obey what God says, which is what God planned to happen to them.

[9]But you are a chosen people, royal priests, a holy nation, a people for God's own possession. You were chosen to tell about the wonderful acts of God, who called you out of darkness into his wonderful light. [10]At one time you were not a people, but now you are God's people. In the past you had never received mercy, but now you have received God's mercy.

NKJV

God through Jesus Christ. [6]Therefore it is also contained in the Scripture,

> "Behold, I lay in Zion
> A chief cornerstone, elect, precious,
> And he who believes on Him will
> by no means be put to shame."

[7]Therefore, to you who believe, *He is* precious; but to those who are disobedient,

> "The stone which the builders rejected
> Has become the chief cornerstone,"

[8]and

> "A stone of stumbling
> And a rock of offense."

They stumble, being disobedient to the word, to which they also were appointed.

[9]But you *are* a chosen generation, a royal priesthood, a holy nation, His own special people, that you may proclaim the praises of Him who called you out of darkness into His marvelous light; [10]who once *were* not a people but *are* now the people of God, who had not obtained mercy but now have obtained mercy.

DISCOVERY

Explore the Bible reading by discussing these questions.

2. How can we grow in our faith?

_____

_____

_____

3. Why does Scripture call us "living stones"?

_____

_____

_____

4. List several characteristics of Christ as the Cornerstone.

_____

_____

_____

5. How could Christ cause someone to stumble?

_____

_____

_____

6. What special role has God given to us because we are Christians?

_____

_____

_____

INSPIRATION

Here is an uplifting thought from *The Inspirational Study Bible*.

Can you still remember? Are you still in love with Him? . . . Remember Jesus. Before you remember anything, remember Him. If you forget anything, don't forget Him.

Oh, but how quickly we forget. So much happens through the years. So many changes within. So many alterations without. And, somewhere, back there, we leave Him. We don't turn away from Him . . . we just don't take Him with us. Assignments come. Promotions come. Budgets are made. Kids are born, and the Christ . . . the Christ is forgotten.

Has it been a while since you stared at the heavens in speechless amazement? Has it been a while since you realized God's divinity and your carnality?

If it has, then you need to know something. He is still there. He hasn't left. Under all those papers and books and reports and years. In the midst of all those voices and faces and memories and pictures, He is still there.

(From *Six Hours One Friday*
by Max Lucado)

RESPONSE

Use these questions to share more deeply with each other.

7. Think about the enthusiasm and commitment you had for Christ when you first became a follower of His. Why is that level of enthusiasm and commitment difficult to maintain?

_____

_____

_____

8. How can we rekindle our first love for Jesus?

_____

_____

_____

9. In what way can we nourish our commitment to Christ so that it will not diminish over time?

_____

_____

_____

PRAYER

God, forgive us for the times we have left you behind in our struggle to get ahead. Forgive us for forgetting who you are and what you have done for us. We know that you have been there—always waiting, always hoping, and always ready to forgive. May we understand what it means to make you the Cornerstone of our lives.

JOURNALING

Take a few moments to record your personal insights from this lesson.

How would I compare my commitment to Christ from when I first believed until now?

ADDITIONAL QUESTIONS

10. How can you determine whether Jesus is the Cornerstone on which your life is built?

_____

_____

_____

11. List some ways your daily life is different because of your relationship with Jesus.

_____

_____

_____

12. How does this passage reaffirm your sense of worth and value in God's eyes?

_____

_____

_____

For more Bible passages on Christ, the Cornerstone, see Psalm 118:21–24; Matthew 21:42–43; Acts 4:10–12; Ephesians 2:19–22.

To complete the Books of 1 & 2 Peter during this twelve-part study, read 1 Peter 2:1–10.

ADDITIONAL THOUGHTS

LESSON FOUR

FOLLOWING JESUS' EXAMPLE

REFLECTION

Begin your study by sharing thoughts on this question.

1. Think of a fellow believer whom you greatly admire. In what ways would you like to model your life after that person's example?

_____

_____

_____

BIBLE READING

Read 1 Peter 2:11–25 from the NCV or the NKJV.

NCV

[11]Dear friends, you are like foreigners and strangers in this world. I beg you to avoid the evil things your bodies want to do that fight against your soul. [12]People who do not believe are living all around you and might say that you are doing wrong. Live such good lives that they will see the good things you do and will give glory to God on the day when Christ comes again.

[13]For the Lord's sake, yield to the people who have authority in this world: the king, who is

NKJV

[11]Beloved, I beg _you_ as sojourners and pilgrims, abstain from fleshly lusts which war against the soul, [12]having your conduct honorable among the Gentiles, that when they speak against you as evildoers, they may, by _your_ good works which they observe, glorify God in the day of visitation.

[13]Therefore submit yourselves to every ordinance of man for the Lord's sake, whether to the king as supreme, [14]or to governors, as to those who are sent by him for the punishment

NCV

the highest authority, [14]and the leaders who are sent by him to punish those who do wrong and to praise those who do right. [15]It is God's desire that by doing good you should stop foolish people from saying stupid things about you. [16]Live as free people, but do not use your freedom as an excuse to do evil. Live as servants of God. [17]Show respect for all people: Love the brothers and sisters of God's family, respect God, honor the king.

[18]Slaves, yield to the authority of your masters with all respect, not only those who are good and kind, but also those who are dishonest. [19]A person might have to suffer even when it is unfair, but if he thinks of God and stands the pain, God is pleased. [20]If you are beaten for doing wrong, there is no reason to praise you for being patient in your punishment. But if you suffer for doing good, and you are patient, then God is pleased. [21]This is what you were called to do, because Christ suffered for you and gave you an example to follow. So you should do as he did.

[22]"He had never sinned,
    and he had never lied."

[23]People insulted Christ, but he did not insult them in return. Christ suffered, but he did not threaten. He let God, the One who judges rightly, take care of him. [24]Christ carried our sins in his body on the cross so we would stop living for sin and start living for what is right. And you are healed because of his wounds. [25]You were like sheep that wandered away, but now you have come back to the Shepherd and Protector of your souls.

NKJV

of evildoers and *for the* praise of those who do good. [15]For this is the will of God, that by doing good you may put to silence the ignorance of foolish men— [16]as free, yet not using liberty as a cloak for vice, but as bondservants of God. [17]Honor all *people*. Love the brotherhood. Fear God. Honor the king.

[18]Servants, *be* submissive to *your* masters with all fear, not only to the good and gentle, but also to the harsh. [19]For this *is* commendable, if because of conscience toward God one endures grief, suffering wrongfully. [20]For what credit *is it* if, when you are beaten for your faults, you take it patiently? But when you do good and suffer, if you take it patiently, this *is* commendable before God. [21]For to this you were called, because Christ also suffered for us, leaving us an example, that you should follow His steps:

[22]"Who committed no sin,
    Nor was deceit found in His mouth";

[23]who, when He was reviled, did not revile in return; when He suffered, He did not threaten, but committed *Himself* to Him who judges righteously; [24]who Himself bore our sins in His own body on the tree, that we, having died to sins, might live for righteousness—by whose stripes you were healed. [25]For you were like sheep going astray, but have now returned to the Shepherd and Overseer of your souls.

DISCOVERY

Explore the Bible reading by discussing these questions.

2. Why didn't Jesus feel any need to seek revenge?

_____

_____

_____

3. Why is it important for us to lead good lives?

_____

_____

_____

4. Why should we yield to authorities?

_____

_____

_____

5. What happens when believers endure suffering for doing good?

_____

_____

_____

6. What can we learn from Jesus about responding to unfair treatment?

_____

_____

_____

INSPIRATION

Here is an uplifting thought from *The Inspirational Study Bible*.

The disciples are annoyed. As Jesus sits in silence, they grow more smug. "Send her away," they demand. The spotlight is put on Jesus. He looks at the disciples, then looks at the woman. And what follows is one of the most intriguing dialogues in the New Testament.

"I was sent only to the lost sheep of Israel," he says.

"Lord, help me!"

"It is not right to take the children's bread and toss it to their dogs," he answers.

"But even the dogs eat the crumbs that fall from their masters' tables," she responds.

Is Jesus being rude? Is he worn-out? Is he frustrated? Is he calling this woman a dog? How do we explain this dialogue? . . .

Could it be that Jesus' tongue is poking his cheek? Could it be that he and the woman are engaging in satirical banter? Is it wry exchange in which God's unlimited grace is being highlighted? Could Jesus be so delighted to have found one who is not bartering with a religious system or proud of a heritage that he can't resist a bit of satire?

He knows he can heal her daughter. He knows he isn't bound by a plan. He knows her heart is good. So he decides to engage in a humorous moment with a faithful woman. In essence, here's what they said:

"Now, you know that God only cares about Jews," he says smiling.

And when she catches on, she volleys back, "But your bread is so precious, I'll be happy to eat the crumbs."

In a spirit of exuberance, he bursts out, "Never have I seen such faith! Your daughter is healed."

This story does not portray a contemptuous God. It portrays a willing One who delights in a sincere seeker.

Aren't you glad he does?

(From *In the Eye of the Storm*
by Max Lucado)

RESPONSE

Use these questions to share more deeply with each other.

7. How do we tend to react when others hurt us?

_____

_____

_____

8. In what way does Christ's example affect the way you view your problems and pain?

_____

_____

_____

9. How can our emotional wounds interfere with our spiritual growth?

_____

_____

_____

PRAYER

Father, sometimes the urge to seek revenge seems too strong to resist. Even though we have experienced your great mercy and love, we refuse to extend your grace to others. Forgive us, Father, for choosing to retaliate, instead of forgive. Remind us of how you dealt with injustice and unfairness when you were on earth, and give us the strength to follow your example.

JOURNALING

Take a few moments to record your personal insights from this lesson.

Who do I need to forgive?

ADDITIONAL QUESTIONS

10. In what circumstances is it tempting to retaliate?

_____

_____

_____

11. When has God helped you forgive someone who hurt you deeply?

_____

_____

_____

12. How can you fight the urge to get back at people who mistreat you?

_____

_____

_____

For more Bible passages on following Jesus' example, see John 8:12; 12:26; 13:15; 1 Corinthians 11:1; Ephesians 5:1–2; 1 Thessalonians 1:6.

To complete the Books of 1 & 2 Peter during this twelve-part study, read 1 Peter 2:11–25.

ADDITIONAL THOUGHTS

LESSON FIVE

HOLY LIVING

REFLECTION

Begin your study by sharing thoughts on this question.

1. Think of someone who displays inner strength and beauty. What have you learned from that person?

_____

_____

_____

BIBLE READING

Read 1 Peter 3:1–7 from the NCV or the NKJV.

NCV

¹In the same way, you wives should yield to your husbands. Then, if some husbands do not obey God's teaching, they will be persuaded to believe without anyone's saying a word to them. They will be persuaded by the way their wives live. ²Your husbands will see the pure lives you live with your respect for God. ³It is not fancy hair, gold jewelry, or fine clothes that should make you beautiful. ⁴No, your beauty should come from within you—the beauty of a gentle and quiet spirit that will never be destroyed

NKJV

¹Wives, likewise, *be* submissive to your own husbands, that even if some do not obey the word, they, without a word, may be won by the conduct of their wives, ²when they observe your chaste conduct *accompanied* by fear. ³Do not let your adornment be *merely* outward—arranging the hair, wearing gold, or putting on *fine* apparel— ⁴rather *let it be* the hidden person of the heart, with the incorruptible *beauty* of a gentle and quiet spirit, which is very precious in the sight of God. ⁵For in this manner,

NCV

and is very precious to God. ⁵In this same way the holy women who lived long ago and followed God made themselves beautiful, yielding to their own husbands. ⁶Sarah obeyed Abraham, her husband, and called him her master. And you women are true children of Sarah if you always do what is right and are not afraid.

⁷In the same way, you husbands should live with your wives in an understanding way, since they are weaker than you. But show them respect, because God gives them the same blessing he gives you—the grace that gives true life. Do this so that nothing will stop your prayers.

NKJV

in former times, the holy women who trusted in God also adorned themselves, being submissive to their own husbands, ⁶as Sarah obeyed Abraham, calling him lord, whose daughters you are if you do good and are not afraid with any terror.

⁷Husbands, likewise, dwell with *them* with understanding, giving honor to the wife, as to the weaker vessel, and as *being* heirs together of the grace of life, that your prayers may not be hindered.

DISCOVERY

Explore the Bible reading by discussing these questions.

2. How can believing wives win their unbelieving husbands to Christ?

_____

_____

_____

3. Why is inner beauty precious to God?

_____

_____

_____

4. List some ways we can cultivate inner beauty.

_____

_____

_____

5. What can we learn from women, like Sarah, who lived long ago?

_____

_____

_____

6. In what ways do others benefit when believers live holy, pure lives?

_____

_____

_____

INSPIRATION

Here is an uplifting thought from *The Inspirational Study Bible*.

The holiness we are to exhibit is not our own, but the holiness of Christ in us. We are not holy, and we will not become holy humans. Christ in us can manifest His holiness if we will yield our flesh to Him. This is not a human operation; it is a spiritual one. Jesus installs His holiness in us by grace. Not a once-for-all-time transaction, this is a daily, moment-by-moment striving to live more by the Spirit and less by the flesh.

...A friend bought his daughter a new car, but it must sit in the garage until she reaches the legal driving age. Until her sixteenth birthday she only has partial use of the car, when accompanied by an adult. Similarly, holiness is like a gift already purchased for us (by the blood of Christ), but we cannot have full use of it until a certain date in the future (our glorification).

Becoming holy is a process which includes God's part and our part. On one hand, our part is to stay out of God's part—to yield, to surrender, to stop seeking God on our own terms. But our part also is to obey. It is to enter His rehabilitation program.

When you put yourself under a doctor's care, he cannot help you if you don't follow his instructions. As the patient surrenders his own good ideas and obeys the doctor's instruction, he becomes well. The same is true in sanctification. If you and I want to be made holy, then we must willingly surrender ourselves to His care, and we must also actively obey His instructions.

We have no more power to make ourselves holy than a dying man has to save himself. We are weak and tired, and we cannot offer much help. However, we can submit to His rehabilitation program—sanctification. The key to our part is faith—to seek Him in obedience.

(From *Walking with Christ in the Details of Life* by Patrick Morley)

RESPONSE

Use these questions to share more deeply with each other.

7. How can we demonstrate holiness with our lives?

_____

_____

_____

8. Why is it important to realize that becoming holy is a process, not a one-time event?

_____

_____

_____

9. What is God's part and what is our responsibility in the sanctification process?

_____

_____

_____

PRAYER

Father, we want to be holy, but we are weak and prone to sin. Manifest your holiness in us. Help us to surrender our selfish desires to your perfect will. Teach us what it means to live by your Spirit, not our flesh. Persuade others to believe in you through our lives.

JOURNALING

Take a few moments to record your personal insights from this lesson.

What do I need to surrender to God?

ADDITIONAL QUESTIONS

10. Why do we pay more attention to what people do than to what they say?

_____

_____

_____

11. List some ways we focus more on enhancing our outward appearance than developing our inner character.

_____

_____

_____

12. What about our lives will attract people to Christ?

_____

_____

_____

For more Bible passages on holy living, see Leviticus 11:44–45; 1 Corinthians 1:2, 30; 1 Thessalonians 4:3–7; 2 Timothy 1:8–9; Hebrews 10:10–14; 1 Peter 1:14–16; 2 Peter 3:11.

To complete the Books of 1 & 2 Peter during this twelve-part study, read 1 Peter 3:1–7.

ADDITIONAL THOUGHTS

LESSON SIX

LOVING PEOPLE

REFLECTION

Begin your study by sharing thoughts on this statement.

1. Describe a time when someone demonstrated Christ's love to you in a practical way.

_____

_____

_____

BIBLE READING

Read 1 Peter 3:8–22 from the NCV or the NKJV.

NCV

⁸Finally, all of you should be in agreement, understanding each other, loving each other as family, being kind and humble. ⁹Do not do wrong to repay a wrong, and do not insult to repay an insult. But repay with a blessing, because you yourselves were called to do this so that you might receive a blessing. ¹⁰The Scripture says,

"A person must do these things
    to enjoy life and have many happy
      days.

NKJV

⁸Finally, all of *you be* of one mind, having compassion for one another; love as brothers, *be* tenderhearted, *be* courteous; ⁹not returning evil for evil or reviling for reviling, but on the contrary blessing, knowing that you were called to this, that you may inherit a blessing. ¹⁰For

"He who would love life
    And see good days,
    Let him refrain his tongue from evil,

NCV

He must not say evil things,
  and he must not tell lies.
[11] He must stop doing evil and do good.
  He must look for peace and work for it.
[12] The Lord sees the good people
  and listens to their prayers.
But the Lord is against
  those who do evil."

[13] If you are trying hard to do good, no one can really hurt you. [14] But even if you suffer for doing right, you are blessed.

  "Don't be afraid of what they fear;
  do not dread those things."

[15] But respect Christ as the holy Lord in your hearts. Always be ready to answer everyone who asks you to explain about the hope you have, [16] but answer in a gentle way and with respect. Keep a clear conscience so that those who speak evil of your good life in Christ will be made ashamed. [17] It is better to suffer for doing good than for doing wrong if that is what God wants. [18] Christ himself suffered for sins once. He was not guilty, but he suffered for those who are guilty to bring you to God. His body was killed, but he was made alive in the spirit. [19] And in the spirit he went and preached to the spirits in prison [20] who refused to obey God long ago in the time of Noah. God was waiting patiently for them while Noah was building the boat. Only a few people—eight in all—were saved by water. [21] And that water is

NKJV

  And his lips from speaking deceit.
[11] Let him turn away from evil and do good;
  Let him seek peace and pursue it.
[12] For the eyes of the LORD are on the
    righteous,
  And His ears are open to their prayers;
  But the face of the LORD is against those
    who do evil."

[13] And who *is* he who will harm you if you become followers of what is good? [14] But even if you should suffer for righteousness' sake, *you are* blessed. "*And do not be afraid of their threats, nor be troubled.*" [15] But sanctify the Lord God in your hearts, and always *be* ready to *give* a defense to everyone who asks you a reason for the hope that is in you, with meekness and fear; [16] having a good conscience, that when they defame you as evildoers, those who revile your good conduct in Christ may be ashamed. [17] For *it is* better, if it is the will of God, to suffer for doing good than for doing evil.

[18] For Christ also suffered once for sins, the just for the unjust, that He might bring us to God, being put to death in the flesh but made alive by the Spirit, [19] by whom also He went and preached to the spirits in prison, [20] who formerly were disobedient, when once the Divine longsuffering waited in the days of Noah, while *the* ark was being prepared, in which a few, that is, eight souls, were saved through water.

NCV

like baptism that now saves you—not the washing of dirt from the body, but the promise made to God from a good conscience. And this is because Jesus Christ was raised from the dead. ²²Now Jesus has gone into heaven and is at God's right side ruling over angels, authorities, and powers.

NKJV

²¹There is also an antitype which now saves us—baptism (not the removal of the filth of the flesh, but the answer of a good conscience toward God), through the resurrection of Jesus Christ, ²²who has gone into heaven and is at the right hand of God, angels and authorities and powers having been made subject to Him.

DISCOVERY

Explore the Bible reading by discussing these questions.

2. How should we treat each other?

_____

_____

_____

3. When is it most difficult to demonstrate a loving attitude toward others?

_____

_____

_____

4. Describe the kind of person who enjoys life and pleases God.

_____

_____

_____

5. Why is it better to suffer for doing good than for doing wrong?

_____

_____

_____

6. What difference does Christ's resurrection make in how we treat others?

_____

_____

_____

INSPIRATION

Here is an uplifting thought from *The Inspirational Study Bible*.

In our house we call 5:00 p.m. the piranha hour. That's the time of day when everyone wants a piece of Mom. Sara, the baby, is hungry. Andrea wants Mom to read her a book. Jenna wants help with her homework. And I—the ever-loving, ever-sensitive husband—want Denalyn to drop everything and talk to me about my day.

When is your piranha hour? When do people in your world demand much and offer little?

Every boss has had a day in which the requests outnumber the results. There's not a businessperson alive who hasn't groaned as an armada of assignments docks at his or her desk. For the teacher, the piranha hour often begins when the first student enters and ends when the last student leaves.

Piranha hours: parents have them, bosses endure them, secretaries dread them, teachers are besieged by them, and Jesus taught us how to live through them successfully.

When hands extended and voices demanded, Jesus responded with love. He did so because the code within him disarmed the alarm. The code is worth noting: "People are precious."

(From *In the Eye of the Storm* by Max Lucado)

RESPONSE

Use these questions to share more deeply with each other.

7. When is your "piranha hour"?

_____

_____

_____

8. How can we find the strength to love people, even when they have nothing to give in return?

_____

_____

_____

9. In what way can you remind yourself of Christ's example the next time you feel overwhelmed by the demands of others?

_____

_____

_____

PRAYER

Father, when we feel incapable of showing your love to others, when we have nothing left to give, we pray that you would fill us with your grace. During those dry, dark times, Father, we ask that you would give us the strength to love sacrificially. Teach us how to love as you loved. May your mercy and compassion overflow from our hearts to others.

JOURNALING

Take a few moments to record your personal insights from this lesson.

What can I find to value about that one person I need God's help to love more deeply?

ADDITIONAL QUESTIONS

10. What kinds of issues create tension and conflict between believers?

_____

_____

_____

11. What practical steps can we take to promote harmony in the Body of Christ?

_____

_____

_____

12. What does it mean to work for peace?

_____

_____

_____

For more Bible passages on loving people, see Matthew 5:43–48; 22:38–40; John 13:34–35; Romans 12:9–10; 1 Corinthians 13:1–13; Galatians 5:13–14; Colossians 3:14; 1 Thessalonians 4:9–10; Hebrews 10:24; 1 Peter 1:22; 1 John 3:11, 16–18; 4:7–21; 2 John 5–6.

To complete the Books of 1 & 2 Peter during this twelve-part study, read 1 Peter 3:8–22.

ADDITIONAL THOUGHTS

LESSON SEVEN

JOYFUL SERVICE

REFLECTION

Begin your study by sharing thoughts on this question.

1. Think of a time when you found great joy in serving in your church or community. What made that experience joyful?

_____

_____

_____

BIBLE READING

Read 1 Peter 4:1–11 from the NCV or the NKJV.

NCV

¹Since Christ suffered while he was in his body, strengthen yourselves with the same way of thinking Christ had. The person who has suffered in the body is finished with sin. ²Strengthen yourselves so that you will live here on earth doing what God wants, not the evil things people want. ³In the past you wasted too much time doing what nonbelievers enjoy. You were guilty of sexual sins, evil desires, drunkenness, wild and drunken parties, and hateful idol worship. ⁴Nonbelievers think it is strange

NKJV

¹Therefore, since Christ suffered for us in the flesh, arm yourselves also with the same mind, for he who has suffered in the flesh has ceased from sin, ²that he no longer should live the rest of *his* time in the flesh for the lusts of men, but for the will of God. ³For we *have spent* enough of our past lifetime in doing the will of the Gentiles—when we walked in lewdness, lusts, drunkenness, revelries, drinking parties, and abominable idolatries. ⁴In regard to these, they think it strange that you do not run with *them*

NCV

that you do not do the many wild and wasteful things they do, so they insult you. [5]But they will have to explain this to God, who is ready to judge the living and the dead. [6]For this reason the Good News was preached to those who are now dead. Even though they were judged like all people, the Good News was preached to them so they could live in the spirit as God lives.

[7]The time is near when all things will end. So think clearly and control yourselves so you will be able to pray. [8]Most importantly, love each other deeply, because love will cause many sins to be forgiven. [9]Open your homes to each other, without complaining. [10]Each of you has received a gift to use to serve others. Be good servants of God's various gifts of grace. [11]Anyone who speaks should speak words from God. Anyone who serves should serve with the strength God gives so that in everything God will be praised through Jesus Christ. Power and glory belong to him forever and ever. Amen.

NKJV

in the same flood of dissipation, speaking evil of *you*. [5]They will give an account to Him who is ready to judge the living and the dead. [6]For this reason the gospel was preached also to those who are dead, that they might be judged according to men in the flesh, but live according to God in the spirit.

[7]But the end of all things is at hand; therefore be serious and watchful in your prayers. [8]And above all things have fervent love for one another, for "*love will cover a multitude of sins.*" [9]*Be* hospitable to one another without grumbling. [10]As each one has received a gift, minister it to one another, as good stewards of the manifold grace of God. [11]If anyone speaks, *let him speak* as the oracles of God. If anyone ministers, *let him do it* as with the ability which God supplies, that in all things God may be glorified through Jesus Christ, to whom belong the glory and the dominion forever and ever. Amen.

DISCOVERY

Explore the Bible reading by discussing these questions.

2. How can we strengthen ourselves and our gifts?

_____

_____

_____

3. What are the results of loving others?

_____

_____

_____

4. What does it mean to be gifted by God?

_____

_____

_____

5. Think of someone who, in your opinion, used his or her giftedness to serve God. Describe that person.

_____

_____

_____

6. What is the purpose of the gifts and talents God gives us?

_____

_____

_____

INSPIRATION

Here is an uplifting thought from *The Inspirational Study Bible*.

I recently read a story of a woman who for years was married to a harsh husband. Each day he would leave her a list of chores to complete before he returned at the end of the day. "Clean the yard. Stack the firewood. Wash the windows. . . ."

If she didn't complete the tasks, she would be greeted with his explosive anger. But even if she did complete the list, he was never satisfied; he would always find inadequacies in her work.

After several years, the husband passed away. Some time later she remarried, this time to a man who lavished her with tenderness and adoration.

One day, while going through a box of old papers, the wife discovered one of her first husband's lists. And as she read the sheet, a realization caused a tear of joy to splash on the paper.

"I'm still doing all these things, and no one has to tell me. I do it because I love him."

That is the unique characteristic of the new kingdom. Its subjects don't work *in order to* go to heaven; they work because they *are* going to heaven. Arrogance and fear are replaced with gratitude and joy.

(From *The Applause of Heaven*
by Max Lucado)

RESPONSE

Use these questions to share more deeply with each other.

7.   What usually motivates you to serve?

_____

_____

_____

8. In what way does the promise of eternal life impact your attitude toward serving?

_____

_____

_____

9. How can a person find true joy in serving others?

_____

_____

_____

PRAYER

Father, give us a deeper appreciation for what you have done for us and new enthusiasm for serving you. Show us how to extend your love to others. Most importantly, Father, help us to turn to you for wisdom, strength, and perseverance. We give you all the glory for what you will accomplish through us.

JOURNALING

Take a few moments to record your personal insights from this lesson.

What are my gifts and how can I use them to serve others?

ADDITIONAL QUESTIONS

10. What blessings have you received from serving others?

_____

_____

_____

11. How can you depend on God to help you serve, instead of relying on your own strength?

_____

_____

_____

12. In what tangible way can you express your gratitude to God today?

_____

_____

_____

For more Bible passages on serving, see Deuteronomy 10:12; 13:4; Joshua 22:5; Psalm 100:2; Matthew 20:26–28; Romans 12:11; 2 Corinthians 9:12; Galatians 5:13; Ephesians 4:11–13; 6:6–8; Colossians 3:23–24.

To complete the Books of 1 & 2 Peter during this twelve-part study, read 1 Peter 4:1–11.

ADDITIONAL THOUGHTS

LESSON EIGHT

TRUSTING GOD THROUGH TRIALS

REFLECTION

Begin your study by sharing thoughts on this question.

1. Think of a time when God proved his trustworthiness to you. How did that experience stretch your faith?

_____

_____

_____

BIBLE READING

Read 1 Peter 4:12–19 from the NCV or the NKJV.

NCV

¹²My friends, do not be surprised at the terrible trouble which now comes to test you. Do not think that something strange is happening to you. ¹³But be happy that you are sharing in Christ's sufferings so that you will be happy and full of joy when Christ comes again in glory. ¹⁴When people insult you because you follow Christ, you are blessed, because the glorious Spirit, the Spirit of God, is with you. ¹⁵Do not suffer for murder, theft, or any other crime, nor because you trouble other people. ¹⁶But if you

NKJV

¹²Beloved, do not think it strange concerning the fiery trial which is to try you, as though some strange thing happened to you; ¹³but rejoice to the extent that you partake of Christ's sufferings, that when His glory is revealed, you may also be glad with exceeding joy. ¹⁴If you are reproached for the name of Christ, blessed _are you,_ for the Spirit of glory and of God rests upon you. On their part He is blasphemed, but on your part He is glorified. ¹⁵But let none of you suffer as a murderer, a thief, an evildoer, or

NCV

suffer because you are a Christian, do not be ashamed. Praise God because you wear that name. [17]It is time for judgment to begin with God's family. And if that judging begins with us, what will happen to those people who do not obey the Good News of God? [18]"If it is very hard for a good person to be saved,

the wicked person and the sinner will surely be lost!"

[19]So those who suffer as God wants should trust their souls to the faithful Creator as they continue to do what is right.

NKJV

as a busybody in other people's matters. [16]Yet if *anyone suffers* as a Christian, let him not be ashamed, but let him glorify God in this matter.

[17]For the time *has come* for judgment to begin at the house of God; and if *it begins* with us first, what will *be* the end of those who do not obey the gospel of God? [18]Now

" If the righteous one is scarcely saved,
 Where will the ungodly and the sinner appear?"

[19]Therefore let those who suffer according to the will of God commit their souls *to Him* in doing good, as to a faithful Creator.

DISCOVERY

Explore the Bible reading by discussing these questions.

2. In what ways does God test us?

_____

_____

_____

3. How can we share in Christ's sufferings?

_____

_____

_____

4. Why should we rejoice in difficult circumstances?

_____

_____

_____

5. What kind of suffering does God want us to avoid, and what kind does he want us to welcome?

_____

_____

_____

6. In what way can suffering be a blessing?

_____

_____

_____

INSPIRATION

Here is an uplifting thought from *The Inspirational Study Bible*.

Is there anything more frail than a bruised reed? Look at the bruised reed at the water's edge. A once slender and tall stalk of sturdy river grass, it is now bowed and bent.

Are you a bruised reed? Was it so long ago that you stood so tall, so proud? You were upright and sturdy, nourished by the waters and rooted in the riverbed of confidence.

Then something happened. You were bruised . . .

> by harsh words
> by a friend's anger
> by a spouse's betrayal
> by your own failure
> by religion's rigidity.

And you were wounded, bent ever so slightly. Your hollow reed, once erect, now stooped, and hidden in the bulrush.

And the smoldering wick on the candle. Is there anything closer to death than a smoldering wick? Once aflame, now flickering and failing. Still warm from yesterday's passion, but no fire. Not yet cold, but far from hot. Was it that long ago you blazed with faith? Remember how you illuminated the path?

Then came the wind . . . the cold wind, the harsh wind. They said your ideas were foolish. They told you your dreams were too lofty. They scolded you for challenging the time-tested.

The constant wind wore down upon you. Oh, you stood strong for a moment (or maybe a lifetime), but the endless blast whipped your flickering flame, leaving you one pinch away from darkness.

The bruised reed and the smoldering wick. Society knows what to do with you. The world has a place for the beaten. The world will break you off; the world will snuff you out.

But the artists of Scripture proclaim that God won't. Painted on canvas after canvas is the tender touch of a Creator who has a special place for the bruised and weary of the world. A God who is the friend of the wounded heart. A God who is the keeper of your dreams.

(From *He Still Moves Stones*
by Max Lucado)

RESPONSE

Use these questions to share more deeply with each other.

7. What hope is there for those of us who are emotionally wounded?

_____

_____

_____

8. What can we do to develop a faith that will withstand pressure and persecution?

_____

_____

_____

9. Is there any way God has used pain and suffering in your life for the good?

_____

_____

_____

PRAYER

Father, you never said that this life would be easy. Instead, you warned us to expect pain and troubles. But you also promised that you would be with us. O Father, teach us to rely on you, so that we can withstand the struggles and storms that come our way. And even when we cannot understand why you are allowing us to suffer, help us to trust you.

JOURNALING

Take a few moments to record your personal insights from this lesson.

How can I thank God for the trials in my life?

ADDITIONAL QUESTIONS

10. In what ways have you suffered because of your faith in Jesus Christ?

_____

_____

_____

11. Why should we not be surprised when we experience troubles?

_____

_____

_____

12. In practical terms, how can you trust God to help you through difficult times in your life?

_____

_____

_____

For more Bible passages on trials, see Acts 5:41; Romans 5:3; 8:17–18; 2 Corinthians 1:5–7; Philippians 1:29; 3:10; 1 Thessalonians 3:3–4; 2 Thessalonians 1:3–4; 2 Timothy 1:8; Hebrews 12:10–11; James 1:2–4; 1 Peter 1:6–7; 2:19–21.

To complete the Books of 1 & 2 Peter during this twelve-part study, read 1 Peter 4:12–19.

ADDITIONAL THOUGHTS

LESSON NINE

HUMILITY

REFLECTION

Begin your study by sharing thoughts on this question.

1. Think of a respected Christian leader in your community. How has that person set a good example for others to follow?

_____

_____

_____

BIBLE READING

Read 1 Peter 5:1–14 from the NCV or the NKJV.

NCV

¹Now I have something to say to the elders in your group. I also am an elder. I have seen Christ's sufferings, and I will share in the glory that will be shown to us. I beg you to ²shepherd God's flock, for whom you are responsible. Watch over them because you want to, not because you are forced. That is how God wants it. Do it because you are happy to serve, not because you want money. ³Do not be like a ruler over people you are responsible for, but be good examples to them. ⁴Then when Christ, the

NKJV

¹The elders who are among you I exhort, I who am a fellow elder and a witness of the sufferings of Christ, and also a partaker of the glory that will be revealed: ²Shepherd the flock of God which is among you, serving as overseers, not by compulsion but willingly, not for dishonest gain but eagerly; ³nor as being lords over those entrusted to you, but being examples to the flock; ⁴and when the Chief Shepherd appears, you will receive the crown of glory that does not fade away.

NCV

Chief Shepherd, comes, you will get a glorious crown that will never lose its beauty.

⁵In the same way, younger people should be willing to be under older people. And all of you should be very humble with each other.

"God is against the proud,
but he gives grace to the humble."

⁶Be humble under God's powerful hand so he will lift you up when the right time comes. ⁷Give all your worries to him, because he cares about you.

⁸Control yourselves and be careful! The devil, your enemy, goes around like a roaring lion looking for someone to eat. ⁹Refuse to give in to him, by standing strong in your faith. You know that your Christian family all over the world is having the same kinds of suffering.

¹⁰And after you suffer for a short time, God, who gives all grace, will make everything right. He will make you strong and support you and keep you from falling. He called you to share in his glory in Christ, a glory that will continue forever. ¹¹All power is his forever and ever. Amen.

¹²I wrote this short letter with the help of Silas, who I know is a faithful brother in Christ. I wrote to encourage you and to tell you that this is the true grace of God. Stand strong in that grace.

¹³The church in Babylon, who was chosen like you, sends you greetings. Mark, my son in Christ, also greets you. ¹⁴Give each other a kiss of Christian love when you meet.

Peace to all of you who are in Christ.

NKJV

⁵Likewise you younger people, submit yourselves to *your* elders. Yes, all of *you* be submissive to one another, and be clothed with humility, for

"God resists the proud,
But gives grace to the humble."

⁶Therefore humble yourselves under the mighty hand of God, that He may exalt you in due time, ⁷casting all your care upon Him, for He cares for you.

⁸Be sober, be vigilant; because your adversary the devil walks about like a roaring lion, seeking whom he may devour. ⁹Resist him, steadfast in the faith, knowing that the same sufferings are experienced by your brotherhood in the world. ¹⁰But may the God of all grace, who called us to His eternal glory by Christ Jesus, after you have suffered a while, perfect, establish, strengthen, and settle *you*. ¹¹To Him *be* the glory and the dominion forever and ever. Amen.

¹²By Silvanus, our faithful brother as I consider him, I have written to you briefly, exhorting and testifying that this is the true grace of God in which you stand.

¹³She who is in Babylon, elect together with *you*, greets you; and *so does* Mark my son. ¹⁴Greet one another with a kiss of love.

Peace to you all who are in Christ Jesus. Amen.

DISCOVERY

Explore the Bible reading by discussing these questions.

2. List some responsibilities of church leaders.

_____

_____

_____

3. In what way does a spirit of humility among believers benefit the church?

_____

_____

_____

4. How does God reward the humble?

_____

_____

_____

5. List some ways God helps us remain faithful to him.

_____

_____

_____

6. What future can God's people anticipate?

_____

_____

_____

INSPIRATION

Here is an uplifting thought from *The Inspirational Study Bible*.

The attitude Christ modeled for us is one that should typify every Christian, whether in pulpit or pew, whether leader of a vast organization or solitary prayer warrior. Not puffed up with self-importance, but poured out for others. . . .

That doesn't mean we shrink from responsibility. God calls each of us to a particular task. But when the temptation of pride comes knocking . . . as it will . . . we must lock the door against it—whatever that takes.

But the toughest question is, How do we know? Because usually the knock is very faint and we don't listen for it. The best protection I have discovered is accountability. Since we all have blind spots, we must, as we mentioned earlier, submit ourselves to those who can see the logs floating in our eyes.

How often does your church governing body review 1 Peter 5:2 with the elders: "Shepherd the flock of God among you, . . . not under compulsion, but voluntarily, according to the will of God; and not for sordid gain, but with eagerness"? Or Paul's first letter to Timothy? We must constantly check each other on how well we are measuring up to the clear biblical requirements of leadership.

(From *The Body* by Charles Colson)

RESPONSE

Use these questions to share more deeply with each other.

7. Why is it difficult to be humble?

_____

_____

_____

8. How can we protect ourselves from the sin of pride?

_____

_____

_____

9. Think of one person to whom you could be accountable in your Christian walk. How could he or she best help you?

_____

_____

_____

PRAYER

Father, thank you for sending your Son to earth to show us how to become servant leaders. Give us the grace to follow his example. Open our eyes to the blind spots in our lives, and help us root out any trace of pride. And Father, thank you for your promise that, at the right time, you will lift up the humble.

JOURNALING

Take a few moments to record your personal insights from this lesson.

Where in my life do I need more humility?

ADDITIONAL QUESTIONS

10. Why is pride a temptation for church leaders?

_____

_____

_____

11. List some signs or evidences of pride.

_____

_____

_____

12. In what practical ways can we humble ourselves?

_____

_____

_____

For more Bible passages on humility, see Proverbs 11:2; 15:33; Zephaniah 2:3; Luke 14:11; Ephesians 4:2; Philippians 2:3; Colossians 3:12; James 4:10.

To complete the Books of 1 & 2 Peter during this twelve-part study, read 1 Peter 5:1–14.

ADDITIONAL THOUGHTS

INTRODUCTION

*I*f a friend warns you, it's one thing. If a doctor warns you, you listen. But if your friend is your doctor, you lean forward and take note.

My friend is my doctor. My doctor is my friend. Most of my physical exams are salted with friendly chatter and jokes. There have been occasions, however, when his tone gets solemn and his voice urgent.

"We're going to have to watch this, Max."

"You haven't been exercising, have you ..."

"With your family's history, you have to watch your diet."

When it's a warning from a friend, you listen.

The second letter from Peter is a warning from a friend. His first letter was a warning about trials from without (persecution). His second caution is a warning about trials from within (heresy).

In this, the last letter we have from him, he urges Christians to be careful. Avoid short-sightedness (1:2–11). Be on guard for false teachers (2:1–22). And, most importantly, be vigilant against personal complacency which will lead to a lazy faith.

The doctor's task is to detect concerns from within and urge you to take caution. Peter's task is the same. Heed his counsel.

LESSON TEN

SELF-DISCIPLINE

REFLECTION

Begin your study by sharing thoughts on this question.

1. What spiritual disciplines have helped you the most in your Christian walk?

_____

_____

_____

BIBLE READING

Read 2 Peter 1:1–21 from the NCV or the NKJV.

NCV

¹From Simon Peter, a servant and apostle of Jesus Christ.

To you who have received a faith as valuable as ours, because our God and Savior Jesus Christ does what is right.

²Grace and peace be given to you more and more, because you truly know God and Jesus our Lord.

³Jesus has the power of God, by which he has given us everything we need to live and to serve God. We have these things because we know him. Jesus called us by his glory and goodness.

NKJV

¹Simon Peter, a bondservant and apostle of Jesus Christ,

To those who have obtained like precious faith with us by the righteousness of our God and Savior Jesus Christ:

²Grace and peace be multiplied to you in the knowledge of God and of Jesus our Lord, ³as His divine power has given to us all things that *pertain* to life and godliness, through the knowledge of Him who called us by glory and

NCV

⁴Through these he gave us the very great and precious promises. With these gifts you can share in being like God, and the world will not ruin you with its evil desires.

⁵Because you have these blessings, do your best to add these things to your lives: to your faith, add goodness; and to your goodness, add knowledge; ⁶and to your knowledge, add self-control; and to your self-control, add patience; and to your patience, add service for God; ⁷and to your service for God, add kindness for your brothers and sisters in Christ; and to this kindness, add love. ⁸If all these things are in you and are growing, they will help you to be useful and productive in your knowledge of our Lord Jesus Christ. ⁹But anyone who does not have these things cannot see clearly. He is blind and has forgotten that he was made clean from his past sins.

¹⁰My brothers and sisters, try hard to be certain that you really are called and chosen by God. If you do all these things, you will never fall. ¹¹And you will be given a very great welcome into the eternal kingdom of our Lord and Savior Jesus Christ.

¹²You know these things, and you are very strong in the truth, but I will always help you remember them. ¹³I think it is right for me to help you remember as long as I am in this body. ¹⁴I know I must soon leave this body, as our Lord Jesus Christ has shown me. ¹⁵I will try my best so that you may be able to remember these things even after I am gone.

¹⁶When we told you about the powerful coming of our Lord Jesus Christ, we were not telling just smart stories that someone

NKJV

virtue, ⁴by which have been given to us exceedingly great and precious promises, that through these you may be partakers of the divine nature, having escaped the corruption *that is* in the world through lust.

⁵But also for this very reason, giving all diligence, add to your faith virtue, to virtue knowledge, ⁶to knowledge self-control, to self-control perseverance, to perseverance godliness, ⁷to godliness brotherly kindness, and to brotherly kindness love. ⁸For if these things are yours and abound, *you will be* neither barren nor unfruitful in the knowledge of our Lord Jesus Christ. ⁹For he who lacks these things is shortsighted, even to blindness, and has forgotten that he was cleansed from his old sins.

¹⁰Therefore, brethren, be even more diligent to make your call and election sure, for if you do these things you will never stumble; ¹¹for so an entrance will be supplied to you abundantly into the everlasting kingdom of our Lord and Savior Jesus Christ.

¹²For this reason I will not be negligent to remind you always of these things, though you know and are established in the present truth. ¹³Yes, I think it is right, as long as I am in this tent, to stir you up by reminding *you,* ¹⁴knowing that shortly I *must* put off my tent, just as our Lord Jesus Christ showed me. ¹⁵Moreover I will be careful to ensure that you always have a reminder of these things after my decease.

¹⁶For we did not follow cunningly devised fables when we made known to you the power and coming of our Lord Jesus Christ, but were eyewitnesses of His majesty. ¹⁷For He received from God the Father honor and glory when

NCV

invented. But we saw the greatness of Jesus with our own eyes. [17]Jesus heard the voice of God, the Greatest Glory, when he received honor and glory from God the Father. The voice said, "This is my Son, whom I love, and I am very pleased with him." [18]We heard that voice from heaven while we were with Jesus on the holy mountain.

[19]This makes us more sure about the message the prophets gave. It is good for you to follow closely what they said as you would follow a light shining in a dark place, until the day begins and the morning star rises in your hearts. [20]Most of all, you must understand this: No prophecy in the Scriptures ever comes from the prophet's own interpretation. [21]No prophecy ever came from what a person wanted to say, but people led by the Holy Spirit spoke words from God.

NKJV

such a voice came to Him from the Excellent Glory: "This is My beloved Son, in whom I am well pleased." [18]And we heard this voice which came from heaven when we were with Him on the holy mountain.

[19]And so we have the prophetic word confirmed, which you do well to heed as a light that shines in a dark place, until the day dawns and the morning star rises in your hearts; [20]knowing this first, that no prophecy of Scripture is of any private interpretation, [21]for prophecy never came by the will of man, but holy men of God spoke *as they were* moved by the Holy Spirit.

DISCOVERY

Explore the Bible reading by discussing these questions.

2. What are the good things we have received from Jesus Christ?

_____

_____

_____

3. List some character traits that we need to work to instill in our own lives.

_____

_____

_____

4. Describe the process it takes to develop these character traits.

_____

_____

_____

5. What confirms to us that we are called and chosen by God?

_____

_____

_____

6. How we can trust what is recorded in Scripture?

_____

_____

_____

INSPIRATION

Here is an uplifting thought from *The Inspirational Study Bible*.

"Add to your faith": Supplement it, flesh it out. Being a Christian doesn't mean believing and then just sitting around. Now that you have faith in God's part, make every effort—that's your part.

That's disciplines.

That's regular "holy habits."

That's pacing yourself for the cross country run to your future.

Says Henri Nouwen, "A spiritual life without discipline is impossible." Tighten your belt. Get tough on yourself. GO FOR IT.

A woman once said to the great Paderewski, "Sir, you are truly a genius."

"Well," he answered, "before I was a genius, I was a drudge!"

To get there, to win—your life needs discipline, order, and arrangement.

"If one examines the secret behind a championship football team, a magnificent orchestra, or a successful business, the principle ingredient is invariably discipline" (James Dobson, *Discipline of the Home*).

You will only discover excellence on the other side of hard work.

(From *My Sacrifice, His Fire*
by Anne Ortlund)

RESPONSE

Use these questions to share more deeply with each other.

7. What does it mean to "add to your faith"?

_____

_____

_____

8. Why is self-discipline (self-control) so important?

_____

_____

_____

9. What results from spiritual discipline?

_____

_____

_____

PRAYER

Father, you know our weaknesses. You know we are prone to be undisciplined in spiritual matters. We need you to come alongside us and help us. We ask you to guide us, and give us perseverance and discipline so that we can grow in our knowledge of you. Let us not be content with less than your best. Show us how much more you want to teach us. May we always hear your voice and obey.

JOURNALING

Take a few moments to record your personal insights from this lesson.

What spiritual discipline do I need to add to my life, and how should I start?

ADDITIONAL QUESTIONS

10. How can a lack of discipline hinder your spiritual growth?

_____

_____

_____

11. What is the difference between being disciplined and being legalistic?

_____

_____

_____

12. What practical steps can you take to become more useful and productive as a Christian?

_____

_____

_____

For more Bible passages on self–discipline (self-control), see Proverbs 1:1–7; 1 Thessalonians 5:6–8; 2 Timothy 1:7; Titus 1:7–8; 2:2–8; 1 Peter 1:13; 4:7.

To complete the Books of 1 & 2 Peter during this twelve-part study, read 2 Peter 1:1–21.

LESSON ELEVEN

FALSE TEACHERS

REFLECTION

Begin your study by sharing thoughts on this question.

1. Think of a time when you were impressed by a dynamic preacher. What do you remember most about his message?

_____

_____

_____

BIBLE READING

Read 2 Peter 2:1–22 from the NCV or the NKJV.

NCV

¹There used to be false prophets among God's people, just as you will have some false teachers in your group. They will secretly teach things that are wrong—teachings that will cause people to be lost. They will even refuse to accept the Master, Jesus, who bought their freedom. So they will bring quick ruin on themselves. ²Many will follow their evil ways and say evil things about the way of truth. ³Those false teachers only want your money, so they will use you by telling you lies. Their

NKJV

¹But there were also false prophets among the people, even as there will be false teachers among you, who will secretly bring in destructive heresies, even denying the Lord who bought them, *and* bring on themselves swift destruction. ²And many will follow their destructive ways, because of whom the way of truth will be blasphemed. ³By covetousness they will exploit you with deceptive words; for a long time their judgment has not been idle, and their destruction does not slumber.

NCV

judgment spoken against them long ago is still coming, and their ruin is certain.

[4]When angels sinned, God did not let them go free without punishment. He sent them to hell and put them in caves of darkness where they are being held for judgment. [5]And God punished the world long ago when he brought a flood to the world that was full of people who were against him. But God saved Noah, who preached about being right with God, and seven other people with him. [6]And God also destroyed the evil cities of Sodom and Gomorrah by burning them until they were ashes. He made those cities an example of what will happen to those who are against God. [7]But he saved Lot from those cities. Lot, a good man, was troubled because of the filthy lives of evil people. [8](Lot was a good man, but because he lived with evil people every day, his good heart was hurt by the evil things he saw and heard.) [9]So the Lord knows how to save those who serve him when troubles come. He will hold evil people and punish them, while waiting for the Judgment Day. [10]That punishment is especially for those who live by doing the evil things their sinful selves want and who hate authority.

These false teachers are bold and do anything they want. They are not afraid to speak against the angels. [11]But even the angels, who are much stronger and more powerful than false teachers, do not accuse them with insults before the Lord. [12]But these people speak against things they do not understand. They are like animals that act without thinking, animals born to be caught and killed. And, like

NKJV

[4]For if God did not spare the angels who sinned, but cast *them* down to hell and delivered *them* into chains of darkness, to be reserved for judgment; [5]and did not spare the ancient world, but saved Noah, *one of* eight *people,* a preacher of righteousness, bringing in the flood on the world of the ungodly; [6]and turning the cities of Sodom and Gomorrah into ashes, condemned *them* to destruction, making *them* an example to those who afterward would live ungodly; [7]and delivered righteous Lot, *who was* oppressed by the filthy conduct of the wicked[8](for that righteous man, dwelling among them, tormented *his* righteous soul from day to day by seeing and hearing *their* lawless deeds)— [9]*then* the Lord knows how to deliver the godly out of temptations and to reserve the unjust under punishment for the day of judgment, [10]and especially those who walk according to the flesh in the lust of uncleanness and despise authority. *They are* presumptuous, self-willed. They are not afraid to speak evil of dignitaries, [11]whereas angels, who are greater in power and might, do not bring a reviling accusation against them before the Lord.

[12]But these, like natural brute beasts made to be caught and destroyed, speak evil of the things they do not understand, and will utterly perish in their own corruption, [13]*and* will receive the wages of unrighteousness, *as* those who count it pleasure to carouse in the daytime. *They are* spots and blemishes, carousing in their own deceptions while they feast with you, [14]having eyes full of adultery and that cannot cease from sin, enticing unstable souls.

NCV

animals, these false teachers will be destroyed. [13]They have caused many people to suffer, so they themselves will suffer. That is their pay for what they have done. They take pleasure in openly doing evil, so they are like dirty spots and stains among you. They delight in trickery while eating meals with you. [14]Every time they look at a woman they want her, and their desire for sin is never satisfied. They lead weak people into the trap of sin, and they have taught their hearts to be greedy. God will punish them! [15]These false teachers left the right road and lost their way, following the way Balaam went. Balaam was the son of Beor, who loved being paid for doing wrong. [16]But a donkey, which cannot talk, told Balaam he was sinning. It spoke with a man's voice and stopped the prophet's crazy thinking.

[17]Those false teachers are like springs without water and clouds blown by a storm. A place in the blackest darkness has been kept for them. [18]They brag with words that mean nothing. By their evil desires they lead people into the trap of sin—people who are just beginning to escape from others who live in error. [19]They promise them freedom, but they themselves are not free. They are slaves of things that will be destroyed. For people are slaves of anything that controls them. [20]They were made free from the evil in the world by knowing our Lord and Savior Jesus Christ. But if they return to evil things and those things control them, then it is worse for them than it was before. [21]Yes, it would be better for them to have never known the right way than to know it and to turn away from the holy teaching that was given to them.

NKJV

They have a heart trained in covetous practices, *and are* accursed children. [15]They have forsaken the right way and gone astray, following the way of Balaam the *son* of Beor, who loved the wages of unrighteousness; [16]but he was rebuked for his iniquity: a dumb donkey speaking with a man's voice restrained the madness of the prophet.

[17]These are wells without water, clouds carried by a tempest, for whom is reserved the blackness of darkness forever.

[18]For when they speak great swelling *words* of emptiness, they allure through the lusts of the flesh, through lewdness, the ones who have actually escaped from those who live in error. [19]While they promise them liberty, they themselves are slaves of corruption; for by whom a person is overcome, by him also he is brought into bondage. [20]For if, after they have escaped the pollutions of the world through the knowledge of the Lord and Savior Jesus Christ, they are again entangled in them and overcome, the latter end is worse for them than the beginning. [21]For it would have been better for them not to have known the way of righteousness, than having known *it,* to turn from the holy commandment delivered to them. [22]But it has happened to them according to the true proverb: "*A dog returns to his own vomit,*" and, "*a sow, having washed, to her wallowing in the mire.*"

NCV | **NKJV**

²²What they did is like this true saying: "A dog goes back to what it has thrown up," and, "After a pig is washed, it goes back and rolls in the mud."

DISCOVERY

Explore the Bible reading by discussing these questions.

2. Why do people follow false teachers?

_____

_____

_____

3. What motivates false teachers to work their way into churches?

_____

_____

_____

4. List several historical events that show God's justice.

_____

_____

_____

5. What kind of tactics do false teachers use to gain followers?

_____

_____

_____

6. Why will there be certain punishment for those who turn others away from God?

_____

_____

_____

INSPIRATION

Here is an uplifting thought from *The Inspirational Study Bible*.

Jesus was warning the people of His day to be on the lookout for gifted leaders who would take advantage of them and lead them astray. They would be men who looked good on the outside but were corrupt on the inside. They would perform well. . . .

To put it bluntly, great preachers are not necessarily great Christians. The same goes for famous gospel singers and best-selling Christian writers. . . .

The best picture of what a Spirit-filled man looks like is Christ. His life was characterized by love, joy, peace, patience, and so on in the midst of a world characterized by just the opposite of those things. He was certainly no wimp. He stood up to His detractors when it was appropriate. But He knew when to be silent as well. He had the courage and wit to take on the intellectuals of His day on their turf according to their terms. He spoke with authority. People, especially children, were attracted to Him. Even sinners loved to be with Him. He was a very secure man. There was nothing pretentious or intimidating about Him. He didn't need those props. And at the end of His life He tackled the toughest account of all—death. And He won!

(From *The Wonderful Spirit-Filled Life*
by Charles Stanley)

RESPONSE

Use these questions to share more deeply with each other.

7. What makes false teachers popular today?

_____

_____

_____

8. How can we recognize false teaching?

_____

_____

_____

9. There are times when we need to confront and expose sin in the life of other believers. What are some guidelines for deciding when that is appropriate?

_____

_____

_____

PRAYER

Heavenly Father, you are a just and fair God. You have promised to judge the wicked and reward the righteous, and we believe that you will keep your word. Please safeguard us from the influence of evil people. Help us to saturate ourselves with the truth of your Word, so that we easily will recognize and expose false teaching. Father, reveal to us your truth, so that we may walk in it.

JOURNALING

Take a few moments to record your personal insights from this lesson.

What practical steps can I take to become a more discerning listener?

ADDITIONAL QUESTIONS

10. Why do we sometimes downplay God's justice and judgment?

_____

_____

_____

11. How is it helpful to know that God has judged evil throughout history?

_____

_____

_____

12. How can you guard against the influence of the sin in the lives of people around you?

_____

_____

_____

For more Bible passages on the dangers of false teachers, see Isaiah 56:10–12; Jeremiah 23:2–4; 50:6; Ezekiel 34:2–10; Matthew 7:15–23; John 10:12–13; Philippians 1:15–17; 1 Timothy 6:3–5.

To complete the Books of 1 & 2 Peter during this twelve-part study, read 2 Peter 2:1–22.

LESSON TWELVE

GOD IS IN CONTROL

REFLECTION

Begin your study by sharing thoughts on this question.

1. Think of a time when you were disappointed in how God answered one of your prayers. Did there come a time when you realized that God's answer was best for you?

_____

_____

_____

BIBLE READING

Read 2 Peter 3:1–18 from the NCV or the NKJV.

NCV

¹My friends, this is the second letter I have written you to help your honest minds remember. ²I want you to think about the words the holy prophets spoke in the past, and remember the command our Lord and Savior gave us through your apostles. ³It is most important for you to understand what will happen in the last days. People will laugh at you. They will live doing the evil things they want to do. ⁴They will say, "Jesus promised to come again. Where is

NKJV

¹Beloved, I now write to you this second epistle (in *both of* which I stir up your pure minds by way of reminder), ²that you may be mindful of the words which were spoken before by the holy prophets, and of the commandment of us, the apostles of the Lord and Savior, ³knowing this first: that scoffers will come in the last days, walking according to their own lusts, ⁴and saying, "Where is the promise of His coming? For since the fathers

NCV

he? Our fathers have died, but the world continues the way it has been since it was made." ⁵But they do not want to remember what happened long ago. By the word of God heaven was made, and the earth was made from water and with water. ⁶Then the world was flooded and destroyed with water. ⁷And that same word of God is keeping heaven and earth that we now have in order to be destroyed by fire. They are being kept for the Judgment Day and the destruction of all who are against God.

⁸But do not forget this one thing, dear friends: To the Lord one day is as a thousand years, and a thousand years is as one day. ⁹The Lord is not slow in doing what he promised— the way some people understand slowness. But God is being patient with you. He does not want anyone to be lost, but he wants all people to change their hearts and lives.

¹⁰But the day of the Lord will come like a thief. The skies will disappear with a loud noise. Everything in them will be destroyed by fire, and the earth and everything in it will be burned up. ¹¹In that way everything will be destroyed. So what kind of people should you be? You should live holy lives and serve God, ¹²as you wait for and look forward to the coming of the day of God. When that day comes, the skies will be destroyed with fire, and everything in them will melt with heat. ¹³But God made a promise to us, and we are waiting for a new heaven and a new earth where goodness lives.

¹⁴Dear friends, since you are waiting for this to happen, do your best to be without sin and without fault. Try to be at peace with God. ¹⁵Remember that we are saved because our Lord is

NKJV

fell asleep, all things continue as *they were* from the beginning of creation." ⁵For this they willfully forget: that by the word of God the heavens were of old, and the earth standing out of water and in the water, ⁶by which the world *that* then existed perished, being flooded with water. ⁷But the heavens and the earth *which* are now preserved by the same word, are reserved for fire until the day of judgment and perdition of ungodly men.

⁸But, beloved, do not forget this one thing, that with the Lord one day *is* as a thousand years, and a thousand years as one day. ⁹The Lord is not slack concerning *His* promise, as some count slackness, but is longsuffering toward us, not willing that any should perish but that all should come to repentance.

¹⁰But the day of the Lord will come as a thief in the night, in which the heavens will pass away with a great noise, and the elements will melt with fervent heat; both the earth and the works that are in it will be burned up. ¹¹Therefore, since all these things will be dissolved, what manner *of persons* ought you to be in holy conduct and godliness, ¹²looking for and hastening the coming of the day of God, because of which the heavens will be dissolved, being on fire, and the elements will melt with fervent heat? ¹³Nevertheless we, according to His promise, look for new heavens and a new earth in which righteousness dwells.

¹⁴Therefore, beloved, looking forward to these things, be diligent to be found by Him in peace, without spot and blameless; ¹⁵and consider *that* the longsuffering of our Lord *is* salvation—as also our beloved brother Paul,

NCV

patient. Our dear brother Paul told you the same thing when he wrote to you with the wisdom that God gave him. [16]He writes about this in all his letters. Some things in Paul's letters are hard to understand, and people who are ignorant and weak in faith explain these things falsely. They also falsely explain the other Scriptures, but they are destroying themselves by doing this.

[17]Dear friends, since you already know about this, be careful. Do not let those evil people lead you away by the wrong they do. Be careful so you will not fall from your strong faith. [18]But grow in the grace and knowledge of our Lord and Savior Jesus Christ. Glory be to him now and forever! Amen.

NKJV

according to the wisdom given to him, has written to you, [16]as also in all his epistles, speaking in them of these things, in which are some things hard to understand, which untaught and unstable *people* twist to their own destruction, as *they do* also the rest of the Scriptures.

[17]You therefore, beloved, since you know *this* beforehand, beware lest you also fall from your own steadfastness, being led away with the error of the wicked; [18]but grow in the grace and knowledge of our Lord and Savior Jesus Christ.

To Him *be* the glory both now and forever. Amen.

DISCOVERY

Explore the Bible reading by discussing these questions.

2. Why is it important for us to know what to expect in the last days?

_____

_____

_____

3. Explain why God is delaying his punishment of the wicked.

_____

_____

_____

4. How can we be sure that God is in control?

_____

_____

_____

5. In light of Christ's imminent return, describe how we should live our lives.

_____

_____

_____

6. How can believers guard their faith?

_____

_____

_____

INSPIRATION

Here is an uplifting thought from *The Inspirational Study Bible*.

Be honest. Are we glad he says no to what we want and yes to what we need? Not always. If we ask for a new marriage, and he says honor the one you've got, we aren't happy. If we ask for healing, and he says learn through the pain, we aren't happy. If we ask for more money, and he says treasure the unseen, we aren't always happy.

When God doesn't do what we want, it's not easy. Never has been. Never will be. But faith is the conviction that God knows more than we do about this life and he will get us through it.

Remember, disappointment is caused by unmet expectations. Disappointment is cured by revamped expectations.

I like that story about the fellow who went to the pet store in search of a singing parakeet. Seems he was a bachelor and his house was too quiet. The store owner had just the bird for him, so the man bought it. The next day the bachelor came home from work to a house full of music. He went to the cage to feed the bird and noticed for the first time that the parakeet had only one leg.

He felt cheated that he'd been sold a one-legged bird, so he called and complained.

"What do you want," the store owner responded, "a bird who can sing or a bird who can dance?" . . .

We need to hear that God is still in control. We need to hear that it's not over until he says so. We need to hear that life's mishaps and tragedies are not a reason to bail out. They are simply a reason to sit tight.

Corrie ten Boom used to say, "When the train goes through a tunnel and the world gets dark, do you jump out? Of course not. You sit still and trust the engineer to get you through." . . .

Next time you're disappointed, don't panic. Don't jump out. Don't give up. Just be patient and let God remind you he's still in control. It ain't over till it's over.

(From *He Still Moves Stones* by Max Lucado)

RESPONSE

Use these questions to share more deeply with each other.

7. In what circumstances is it tempting to give up on God?

_____

_____

_____

8. What are the dangers of unrealistic expectations?

_____

_____

_____

9. How do the promises in this passage build up your faith and confidence in God?

_____

_____

_____

PRAYER

Father in heaven, forgive us for demanding that you answer our prayers like we want them to be answered. Help us to be patient and to remember that you are in control. Teach us to surrender our burdens to you, and leave them at your feet. And Father, we thank you that you always do what is best for us.

JOURNALING

Take a few moments to record your personal insights from this lesson.

In what areas of my life have I doubted that God had my best interests at heart?

ADDITIONAL QUESTIONS

10. Why do we sometimes turn away from God when we need him the most?

_____

_____

_____

11. How can you remind yourself of the truth of this passage the next time you feel disappointed or discouraged?

_____

_____

_____

12. What step of faith can you take to demonstrate your renewed trust in God?

_____

_____

_____

For more Bible passages on trusting God, see Psalm 4:5; 20:7; 62:8; Proverbs 3:5; Isaiah 12:2; Nahum 1:7; Zephaniah 3:12; John 14:1–3; Acts 14:23; Hebrews 2:13.

To complete the Books of 1 & 2 Peter during this twelve-part study, read 2 Peter 3:1–18.

ADDITIONAL THOUGHTS

ADDITIONAL THOUGHTS

LEADERS' NOTES

LESSON ONE

Question 1: If you can, think of some times in your own life when you felt hopeless. Try to include a time when you weren't involved in a tragedy, but the situation felt hopeless to you. Help your class to open up about situations that felt hopeless to them, while they may not have appeared tragic to others.

Question 3: You may want to follow this question with questions such as, "What do we have as saved people that we did not have before?" Use 2 Corinthians 5:17 and Titus 3:3–7 to prompt conversation.

Question 5: You may want to refer to 1 Thessalonians 1:2–3 and 2 Timothy 2:1–13 in answering this question.

Question 7: You may want to refer to 1 Corinthians 15:54–55 to prompt discussion.

LESSON TWO

Question 2: Take time for testimonies. Ask class members to describe their lives before salvation and the way their lives were different afterwards.

Question 3: Holiness is not just purity and cleanliness; it is uniqueness. God is a holy God in that he is the one and only true God. You may want to include this point if it doesn't come into the discussion.

Question 5: You may want to include 1 Corinthians 6:19–20 in this discussion.

Question 8: Jesus explained rebirth to Nicodemus in John 3:1–21. You may want to read this as an example.

LESSON THREE

Question 4: If you have a builder in your group, or if you know a builder, consider inviting him or her to discuss the cornerstone from a construction perspective.

Question 7: In Revelation Jesus rebukes a church for losing its first love. You may want to open this question with that passage: Revelation 2:1–5.

LESSON FOUR

Question 2: Before reading this question you may want to read an additional passage about Christ's willingness to suffer—Isaiah 53.

Question 5: Some additional passages to explore include Matthew 5:11–12, Romans 5:1–5, James 5:10–11.

Question 6: In discussing this question you may want to review some times when Jesus was unfairly treated in life as well as death. Some examples: He healed a man, but was criticized because it was on the Sabbath (John 5:7–18); several times the Pharisees set out to trick him (Matthew 22:15–21; John 8:2–8).

Question 9: You may prompt this discussion with questions such as, "How do emotional wounds affect our ability to trust? to love? to obey? to hope?"

LESSON FIVE

Question 2: This may be a good time to discuss the particular difficulties spouses of unbelievers encounter.

Question 5: Some key passages on Sarah include Genesis 12:1–5. Brainstorm with your group the difficulties Abraham's (then called Abram) obedience may have caused for Sarah (then called Sarai). She had to leave her home, her friends, her family. She had to suffer hardship and even risk her life because her husband obeyed God.

Question 7: Some additional verses you may want to include in this discussion are Ephesians 4:22–32; 1 Timothy 2:1–4; Hebrews 12:14.

LESSON SIX

Question 3: There could be many angles to this discussion: when you have been hurt, when the person is difficult, when you are sick, when the person is an enemy, when you are bitter, etc. You may want to continue the discussion until you have covered as many angles as possible.

Question 4: If this question makes you think of someone you've known, you may want to open the discussion by telling about that person or telling about an incident you experienced with them.

Question 7: You may want to also include in this discussion what it feels like when everyone wants a piece of you. What are some typical stress reactions for your group members?

Question 8: Consider what bent 1 John 4:19 puts on this discussion.

LESSON SEVEN

Question 2: Ask your group members to identify their own gifts. If they seem shy to do so, ask them if they can identify the spiritual gifts of each other.

Question 6: Some additional Scriptures to use are 1 Corinthians 7:7; 12:4–11; 14:12.

Question 9: You may want to use Philippians 2:1–8 to jumpstart this discussion.

LESSON EIGHT

Question 4: You may want to refer to 1 Peter 2:18–21 and Romans 5:1–5.

Question 6: There may be members of your group who have experienced suffering that they cannot at this time consider in any way a blessing. Allow for that in your discussion. Grief is a process. Make room so that they don't feel that they are not spiritual enough because they can't be glad this very moment for their own suffering.

Question 9: Be prepared to tell about how God has used pain and suffering in your own life for good.

LESSON NINE

Question 3: You may want to spend time talking about the definition of humility and the traits of humility before this discussion.

Question 7: Ask for and offer personal examples of situations in which it was difficult to be humble. You may want to refer to Paul's reference to false humility in Colossians 2:18, 23.

LESSON TEN

Question 4: Spend some time in this discussion on the difficulty of recognizing personality traits that cannot be changed but can be compensated for. Also discuss those things about ourselves that are habits and, while we may want to believe we can't change them, God can.

Question 5: It would be interesting to hear some personal anecdotes from your group about times they have felt strongly that God wanted them to do something and how they perceived his direction.

Question 6: Some key Scriptures to include in this discussion are 1 Thessalonians 2:13; 2 Timothy 3:16–17; and Hebrews 4:12.

LESSON ELEVEN

Question 2: To lead into this discussion ask the group for some false teachers they have been aware of in the last few years. Talk about the events surrounding those men or women and what made them attractive to their followers.

Question 3: Several of Paul's letters are written to refute false teaching and false teachers. You may want to refer to 2 Corinthians 11:3–15, Galatians 2:1–5; 1 Timothy 6:3–5.

Question 6: Ask for personal examples from the lives of your group members who may not have been classified as false teachers, but who discouraged them in their faith.

Question 9: If you or any of your group members have had to confront a false teacher, take time to share your experience.

LESSON TWELVE

Question 2: The balance between preparing for Christ's return and investing in life now may become a part of your discussion. If you have group members who spend a lot of time estimating the time of Christ's return and others who don't, you may need to emphasize that we all need a balance between living for the future and investing in today. (Part of the reason that Paul wrote the Book of 2 Thessalonians was that the people were so caught up in waiting for Christ's arrival that they had quit their jobs and were becoming idle.)

Question 7: You may want to discuss some people from the Bible who could have been tempted to give up on God: Job in his distress, Sarah (Abraham's wife) in her infertility, Hosea as his wife continued to be unfaithful, King David as he was hunted down by Saul.

Question 9: Ask your group members what other promises of Scripture they hold on to in their difficult times.

ADDITIONAL NOTES

ADDITIONAL NOTES

ADDITIONAL NOTES

ADDITIONAL NOTES

ACKNOWLEDGMENTS

Colson, Charles. *The Body,* copyright 1992, Word Inc., Dallas, Texas.

Graham, Billy. *Peace with God*, copyright 1984, Word, Inc., Dallas, Texas.

Lucado, Max. *He Still Moves Stones,* copyright 1993, Word Inc., Dallas, Texas.

Lucado, Max. *In the Eye of the Storm,* copyright 1991, Word Inc., Dallas, Texas.

Lucado, Max. *On the Anvil*, copyright 1985 by Max Lucado. Used by permission of Tyndale House Publishers, Inc. All rights reserved.

Lucado, Max. *Six Hours One Friday*, Questar Publishers, Multnomah Books, copyright 1989 by Max Lucado.

Lucado, Max. *The Applause of Heaven,* copyright 1990, Word Inc., Dallas, Texas.

Morley, Patrick. *Walking with Christ in the Details of Life*, copyright 1992, Thomas Nelson, Nashville, Tennessee.

Ortlund, Anne. *My Sacrifice, His Fire*, copyright 1991, Word, Inc., Dallas, Texas.

Stanley, Charles. *The Wonderful Spirit-Filled Life*, copyright 1992, Thomas Nelson, Nashville, Tennessee.